The U.S. Armed Forces

The U.S. Army National Guard

by Carrie A. Braulick

Reading Consultant:
Barbara J. Fox
Reading Specialist
North Carolina State University

Capstone
press

Mankato, Minnesota

Blazers is published by Capstone Press,
151 Good Counsel Drive, P.O. Box 669, Mankato, Minnesota 56002.
www.capstonepress.com

Library of Congress Cataloging-in-Publication Data
Braulick, Carrie A., 1975–
    The U.S. Army National Guard / by Carrie A. Braulick.
        p. cm.—(Blazers. The U.S. Armed Forces)
    Summary: "Describes the U.S. Army National Guard, including its
members, vehicles, and missions"—Provided by publisher.
    Includes bibliographical references and index.
    ISBN-13: 978-1-4296-0830-5 (hardcover)
    ISBN-10: 1-4296-0830-7 (hardcover)
1. United States—National Guard—Juvenile literature. I. Title. II. Series.
UA42.B67 2008
355.3'70973—dc22   2007001462

Editorial Credits
Angie Kaelberer, editor; Juliette Peters, set designer; Kyle Grenz, book designer;
    Jo Miller, photo researcher

Photo Credits
Air National Guard photo by Master Sgt. Rob Trubia, 13
AP/Wide World Photos/Ric Feld, 8
Corbis/Reuters/Marc Serota, 7; San Francisco Chronicle/Craig Lee, 11
DVIC/Kaye Richey, 23; MSGT Patrick J. Cashin, 25; PH1(AW) Brien Aho, 5;
    SSGT D. Myles Cullen, 20–21; SSGT Douglas Nicodemus, cover
    (background); TSGT Cheresa D. Theiral, 24; TSGT Dawn M. Price,
    cover (foreground); TSGT Steve Faulisi, 19
The National Guard Image Gallery, 14
Photo by Air Force Senior Master Sgt. Mike Arellano, 9
Photo by Capt. Chris Heathscott, Arkansas National Guard State Public Affairs
    Office, 17
Photo by Ted Carlson/Fotodynamics, 16
U.S. Air Force photo by Master Sgt. Scott Wagers, 27
U.S. Army photo by Pvt. 1st Class Monette Wesolek, 18; SGT Arthur Hamilton,
    28–29; Sgt. Michael J. Carden, 26

**Capstone Press thanks the National Guard Bureau Public Affairs Department
for its assistance with this book.**

1 2 3 4 5 6 12 11 10 09 08 07

Table of Contents

National Guard to the Rescue

After Hurricane Katrina, the people of New Orleans were in trouble. Homes and businesses were in ruins. Water was unsafe to drink. Mud and trash were everywhere.

The governor called the state's National Guard units into action. Within hours, soldiers arrived to help.

BLAZER FACT

The National Guard
traces its history back
to 1636, when colonists
formed citizen militias.

The Guard soldiers searched for survivors and treated injured victims. They handed out food and bottled water. Their quick action saved lives.

Always Ready

Guard members work part-time for the National Guard. They help people after natural disasters. They also fight alongside the full-time Army during wars.

★★★★★★★★★★★★★

The National Guard is always ready for duty. Units meet for training at least one weekend each month and two weeks each year. They practice the skills they need in emergencies.

BLAZER FACT

State governors command Guard units. But the United States president can also call them to action.

M2 machine gun

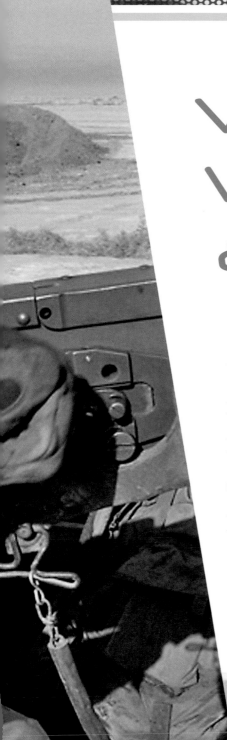

Vehicles, Weapons, and Gear

Army National Guard units use the same equipment as the full-time Army. They drive huge Humvees and M1 tanks. They shoot powerful weapons like the M2 machine gun.

CH-47D Chinook

Helicopters are the best vehicles for many National Guard jobs. The mighty Chinook is big enough to move a Humvee. The speedy Black Hawk is perfect for rescues.

BLAZER FACT

The CH-47D Chinook holds 26,000 pounds (11,800 kilograms) of cargo.

UH-60 Black Hawk

17

Guard members use radios
to communicate. Night vision
goggles and infrared equipment
help them find victims. Infrared
equipment detects body heat.

Night vision goggles

19

UH-60 Black Hawk

Rotor blade

Tail rotor

Main rotor head

Cockpit

Cabin

Faces of the Guard

Each National Guard soldier trains for a certain job. Army Guard jobs include infantry soldiers, pilots, nurses, and police officers.

Some National Guard members serve in the special forces. These soldiers train hard to survive in all kinds of conditions.

National Guard soldiers are always ready to serve their country. Whether fighting terrorists or helping disaster victims, these soldiers have the skills to get the job done.

DANGER
خطر
STAY BACK

BLAZER FACT
In 2005, 50 percent of U.S. forces in Iraq were National Guard and other part-time soldiers.

26

National Guard Ranks

★ ★ ★ ★ ★ ★ ★ ★ ★ ★ ★ ★ ★ ★ ★ ★ ★ ★

ENLISTED	OFFICERS
Private	Lieutenant
Specialist	Captain
Corporal	Major
Sergeant	Lieutenant
Staff Sergeant	Colonel
Sergeant First Class	Colonel
Master Sergeant	General
Sergeant Major	

National Guard on Patrol!

Glossary

disaster (dih-ZASS-tur)—an event that causes much damage or suffering

emergency (i-MUR-juhn-see)—a sudden and dangerous situation that must be handled quickly

infantry (IN-fuhn-tree)—soldiers trained to fight and travel on foot

infrared equipment (in-fruh-RED i-KWIP-muhnt)—gear or machines that detect objects by the heat they give off

militia (muh-LISH-uh)—a group of volunteer citizens who serve as soldiers in emergencies

victim (VIK-tuhm)—a person who is hurt, killed, or made to suffer because of a disaster, accident, or crime

Read More

Barbier, Mary. *The U.S. Army.* America's Armed Forces. Milwaukee: World Almanac Library, 2005.

Braulick, Carrie A. *U.S. Army Helicopters.* Military Vehicles. Mankato, Minn.: Capstone Press, 2006.

Bryan, Nichol. *The National Guard.* Everyday Heroes. Edina, Minn.: Abdo, 2003.

Internet Sites

FactHound offers a safe, fun way to find Internet sites related to this book. All of the sites on FactHound have been researched by our staff.

Here's how:
1. Visit *www.facthound.com*
2. Choose your grade level.
3. Type in this book ID **1429608307** for age-appropriate sites. You may also browse subjects by clicking on letters, or by clicking on pictures and words.
3. Click on the **Fetch It** button.

FactHound will fetch the best sites for you!

Index